Survey of Law School Faculty 2025, Evaluating the Law Review

ISBN 979-8-88517-293-6

Table of contents

Survey of Law School Faculty 2025, Evaluating the Law Review

THE QUESTIONNAIRE

1. Please give us the following contact information:

   A. Name:
   B. Organization:
   C. Title
   D. Email address:

2. You are:

   A. Professor
   B. Assistant/Associate Professor
   C. Lecturer or Research Fellow
   D. Adjunct/Clinical Faculty
   E. Emeritus
   F. Other (please specify)

3. How old are you?

   A. Under 30
   B. 30-39
   C. 40-49
   D. 50-59
   E. 60 or Over

4. Are you male or female?

   A. Male
   B. Female
   C. Transgender

5. Your law school has approximately how many students?

6. Is your law school public or private?

   A. Public
   B. Private

Survey of Law School Faculty 2025, Evaluating the Law Review

7. In the past semester how many courses did you teach?

A. None
B. One
C. Two
D. More than Two

8. Which phrase best approximates the view of your law school taken by organizations that rank law schools?

A. Top 20 law school
B. Somewhere in the 21-75 rank
C. 76 to 250
D. Other

9. Which phrase best characterizes your political beliefs?

A. Right of Conservative
B. Conservative
C. Centrist
D. Liberal
E. Left of Liberal
F. Curriculum Development

10. Your law school's main law review is predominantly run by whom?

A. Students
B. Faculty
C. Other

11. Do you believe that faculty oversight of the student run law review is insufficiently assertive, about right, or assertive enough?

A. Insufficiently assertive
B. About right
C. Assertive enough
D. Not really sure

12. How satisfied are you with the general quality of the law reviews published by your law school?

A. Very satisfied
B. Satisfied
C. Neither satisfied nor dissatisfied
D. Dissatisfied
E. Very dissatisfied

13. What would you do to alter the apparent policies and priorities of your law schools law reviews?

14. Do you believe that ethnic, racial or gender balance should be a consideration in the selection of law school editors?

A. Yes
B. No

15. Have you served in any of the following capacities for any specialty or other type of law review published by your law school?

A. Editor
B. Peer Reviewer
C. Contributor
D. Faculty Advisor

16. About how desirable do you feel it would be to work as a faculty advisor to your law school's main law review?

A. Extremely desirable
B. Very desirable
C. Somewhat desirable
D. Not so desirable
E. Not at all desirable

17. How fair is the selection criteria and process for selecting law review editors from the student body?

A. Very Fair
B. Generally Fair
C. Sometimes Fair
D. Often Unfair
E. Very Unfair

18. What would make your law school's law review better?

19. As best as you can ascertain, how effective is your law school in assuring that the law schools law reviews are effectively marketed and available in various formats and venues?

A. Extremely effective
B. Very effective
C. Somewhat effective
D. Not so effective
E. Not at all effective

Survey of Law School Faculty 2025, Evaluating the Law Review

Characteristics of the sample

Academic title

	#
Professor	61
Assistant/Associate Professor	21
Adjunct/Clinical Faculty	28
Emeritus	15
Other	9
Total	134

Age of respondent

	#
Under 40	6
40-49	19
50-59	33
60 or over	75
Unknown	1
Total	134

Gender of respondent

	#
Male	80
Female	50
Other	4
Total	134

Public or private law school

	#
Public	81
Private	53
Total	134

# of courses taught las semester

	#
None	27
One	40
Two	59
More than two	8
Total	134

Survey of Law School Faculty 2025, Evaluating the Law Review

Law School Self Assessed Ranking

	#
Top 20 law school	27
Somewhere in the 21-75 rank	55
76 to 250	46
Other	6
Total	134

Political views

	#
Conservative	14
Centrist	34
Liberal	65
Left of Liberal	20
Unknown	1
Total	134

Law school enrollment

	#
Less than 400	32
400+ - 550	32
550+ - 800	34
More than 800	36
Total	134

INSTITUTIONAL AFFILIATIONS OF THE SURVEY PARTICIPANTS

Belmont University College of Law
Benjamin N. Cardozo School of Law
Bennett Law Firm
Boston University School of Law
Buffalo State University
Cardozo Law School
Carey Law, U Maryland
Charleston School of Law
Chicago-Kent
Columbia Law School
Creighton University School of Law
Duke Law
Emory University
Fisher Broyles
Fordham University School of Law
Harvard Law School
Howard University
Indiana University
LMU Loyola Law School
Louisiana State Univ. Law Center
LSU Law Center Juvenile Defense Clinic
LSU Law, Tulane Law
Marquette University Law School
MC Law
McGill University
Mercer Univ. School of Law
Mississippi Supreme Court
Mitchell Hamline School of Law
MSU College of Law
New England Law | Boston
Northeastern University School of Law
Northern Illinois University College of Law
Northwestern Law School
OU Law
Pace Law School
Pepperdine Caruso Law
Roger Williams University School of Law
Rutgers Law School
Salesforce, Inc.
Santa Clara University School of Law
Schulich School of Law
SMU Law School
Southern University Law Center
St. Mary's University School of Law
Stetson University College of Law
Temple Law School
The Ohio State University Moritz College of Law

Survey of Law School Faculty 2025, Evaluating the Law Review

The University of Tennessee College of Law
Thomas Jefferson School of Law
Thurgood Marshall S of Law
UCI law
UCLA School of Law
UGA School of Law
UIC Law
UMass Law School
UMKC Law School
UNC-CH
Univ. of Washington School of Law
University of Arkansas
University of California Irvine Law School
University of California San Francisco law
University of Connecticut Law School
University of Florida
University of Georgia School of Law
University of Idaho
University of Illinois Chicago Law School
University of Iowa, College of Law
University of Maryland School of Law
University of Mississippi, School of Law
University of Nebraska - Lincoln College of Law
University of North Carolina School of Law
University of Oklahoma College of Law
University of Oregon School of Law
University of Richmond
University of South Dakota Law School
University of St. Thomas -- Minnesota
University of Tennessee
University of Texas
University of Toronto
University of Tulsa
University of Virginia
University of Wyoming
UT Law and Bush School
UW School of Law
Villanova University
Washington Univ in St Louis
Wayne State University Law School
William S. Boyd School of Law, UNLV
Wise Law Library, CU Boulder
Yale Law School

SUMMARY OF MAIN FINDINGS

Leadership of Law Reviews

Law school faculty overwhelmingly report that their institution's main law review is predominantly student-run, with 89.55% of respondents indicating this. Faculty-run journals are rare, accounting for 3.73%, while 6.72% of respondents did not answer.

Examining law school enrollment, smaller schools (<400 students) are more likely to have faculty involvement (6.25%) compared to larger schools (800+ students), where faculty control is virtually nonexistent (0%). Academic title also plays a role, with 7.14% of adjunct/clinical faculty and 6.67% of emeritus faculty indicating faculty-led law reviews, a higher percentage than full professors (3.28%). Age-wise, younger faculty under 40 were the least likely to report faculty involvement (0%), while those aged 40-49 reported the highest faculty oversight (5.26%). Gender differences are minor, with male and female faculty reporting similar student control rates (88.75% vs. 90.00%). Public law schools show slightly more faculty involvement (4.94%) than private ones (1.89%). Political ideology plays a role as well, with 8.82% of centrists perceiving faculty oversight, compared to 0% of conservatives and left-of-liberal respondents.

Faculty Oversight of Law Reviews

A majority (61.19%) of faculty feel that oversight of student-run law reviews is "about right," while 8.21% believe faculty are insufficiently assertive and 6.72% think oversight is sufficient. A notable 17.16% are unsure.

Breaking this down, larger law schools (550–800 students) are the most likely to find faculty oversight "assertive enough" (14.71%), while smaller schools (<400 students) report the lowest levels of dissatisfaction with oversight (0% saying it is assertive enough). Professors are more likely than assistant/associate professors to find oversight appropriate (65.57% vs. 33.33%), and assistant professors were the most likely to be unsure (33.33%). Political views also show stark differences: 21.43% of conservatives believe faculty oversight is insufficient, while just 3.08% of liberals share that opinion. Public law school faculty are less likely to see oversight as overly assertive (3.70%) compared to private law school faculty (15.09%).

Satisfaction with Law Review Quality

Faculty opinions on law review quality are mixed. While 11.19% are "very satisfied" and 38.06% are "satisfied," a significant portion (32.84%) remain neutral, and 11.94% express dissatisfaction.

Law school size influences perceptions, with larger law schools (800+ students) having the highest dissatisfaction rates (16.67% dissatisfied or very dissatisfied) compared to smaller institutions. Faculty rank also matters: 86.67% of emeritus faculty report satisfaction, while assistant professors are the least satisfied, with just 28.57% expressing positive views. Conservatives are notably more dissatisfied (35.71% dissatisfied or very dissatisfied) compared to liberals (3.08%).

Opinions About Diversity Considerations in Editor Selection

The faculty is divided on whether ethnic, racial, or gender balance should be a factor in selecting law review editors. 31.34% believe it should be considered, while 55.22% oppose it.

Assistant/associate professors are the strongest supporters (52.38% in favor), while emeritus faculty are the most opposed (73.33% against). Political views predict responses, with 78.57% of conservatives against diversity considerations and 55% of left-of-liberal respondents in favor. Women are much more supportive than men (48% vs. 21.25%). Smaller law schools (enrollment <400) are the least likely to support diversity-based selection (9.38% in favor), while medium-sized schools (550-800) are the most likely to favor it (41.18%).

Faculty Participation in Law Reviews

Participation in law reviews is generally low, with only 8.21% of faculty having served as an editor, 17.16% as a peer reviewer, 22.39% as a contributor, and 25.37% as a faculty advisor.

Faculty at top 20 law schools are less involved in editorial roles (14.81% editors, 11.11% peer reviewers, and 11.11% advisors) than those in lower-ranked institutions. Conservatives report the highest participation in contributing articles (64.29%), while left-of-liberal respondents report the lowest (5%). Age also plays a role, with faculty over 60 being the most active contributors (33.33%).

Nearly 41% of full professors have served as a faculty advisor to a law review published by their law school, while this is true of just 4.76% of assistant/associate professors.

Interest in Serving as Law Review Faculty Advisors

Interest in being a faculty advisor is limited, with only 7.47% of faculty rating the role as "extremely" or "very" desirable, while 48.50% find it "not so" or "not at all desirable."

Full professors are the least interested and only 3.28% find the position extremely or very desirable. Assistant professors also show little interest with 42.86% finding it undesirable, while emeritus faculty are the most open to the role (26.67% rate it very/extremely desirable). Age plays a role, with 50% of faculty under 40 saying it is undesirable. Political views also matter—42.86% of conservatives find the role undesirable, compared to 25% of left-of-liberal faculty.

Men are considerably more interested than women; 11.25% of male faculty find the position extremely or very desirable; this is true of only 2% of female faculty. No faculty member from top 20 law schools felt the job was extremely or very desirable.

Opinions on the Fairness of Editor Selection

Faculty generally see the selection process as fair, with 50.75% calling it "generally fair" and 10.45% "very fair." However, 11.94% feel it is "sometimes fair," and 5.23% find it often or very unfair.

Top 20 law school faculty are the most skeptical, with 37.04% failing to answer. Conservatives are the most likely to believe the process is unfair (35.72% saying "sometimes," "often," or "very unfair"), while liberals are the most confident in the process (75.38% rating it fair).

Effectiveness of Law Review Marketing

Most faculty find marketing efforts moderately effective, with 44.78% rating them as "somewhat effective." However, 17.16% say marketing is "very effective" or "extremely effective," while 17.16% find it "not so effective" or "not effective at all."

Older faculty (60+) are the most likely to see marketing as ineffective (18.66%), while those under 40 are the least likely to have an opinion (50% no answer). Top 20 law school faculty are the most critical, with 37.04% providing no response.

Improving the Law Review

Open-ended responses highlight common concerns. The most frequent suggestions for improving law reviews include:

- More Faculty Oversight (25%) – Many faculty believe students lack the experience to make editorial decisions and advocate for more faculty involvement.
- Merit-Based Selection (20%) – Faculty suggest selection should be based on academic performance rather than other factors.
- More Practical Articles (15%) – Some faculty criticize law reviews for being too abstract and disconnected from legal practice.
- More Diversity (10%) – Some respondents want broader representation in selection and topics.
- Better Training for Student Editors (10%) – Concerns about student editors lacking necessary skills in research and writing.

Table 1.1 Your law school's main law review is predominantly run by whom?

	No Answer	Student	Faculty	Other
Entire sample	6.72%	89.55%	3.73%	0.00%

Table 1.2 Your law school's main law review is predominantly run by whom? Broken out by law school enrollment

Law school enrollment	No Answer	Student	Faculty	Other
Less than 400	12.50%	81.25%	6.25%	0.00%
400+ - 550	3.13%	90.63%	6.25%	0.00%
550+ - 800	5.88%	91.18%	2.94%	0.00%
More than 800	5.56%	94.44%	0.00%	0.00%

Table 1.3 Your law school's main law review is predominantly run by whom? Broken out by academic title

Academic title	No Answer	Student	Faculty	Other
Professor	6.56%	90.16%	3.28%	0.00%
Assistant/Associate Professor	9.52%	90.48%	0.00%	0.00%
Adjunct/Clinical Faculty	7.14%	85.71%	7.14%	0.00%
Emeritus	0.00%	93.33%	6.67%	0.00%
Other	11.11%	88.89%	0.00%	0.00%

Table 1.4 Your law school's main law review is predominantly run by whom? Broken out by age of respondent

Age of respondent	No Answer	Student	Faculty	Other
Under 40	16.67%	83.33%	0.00%	0.00%
40-49	10.53%	84.21%	5.26%	0.00%
50-59	0.00%	96.97%	3.03%	0.00%
60 or over	8.00%	88.00%	4.00%	0.00%
Unknown	0.00%	100.00%	0.00%	0.00%

Table 1.5 Your law school's main law review is predominantly run by whom? Broken out by gender of respondent

Gender of respondent	No Answer	Student	Faculty	Other
Male	7.50%	88.75%	3.75%	0.00%
Female	6.00%	90.00%	4.00%	0.00%
Other	0.00%	100.00%	0.00%	0.00%

Table 1.6 Your law school's main law review is predominantly run by whom? Broken out by public or private law school

Public or private law school	No Answer	Student	Faculty	Other
Public	7.41%	87.65%	4.94%	0.00%
Private	5.66%	92.45%	1.89%	0.00%

Table 1.7 Your law school's main law review is predominantly run by whom? Broken out by # of courses taught last semester

# of courses taught last semester	No Answer	Student	Faculty	Other
None	3.70%	96.30%	0.00%	0.00%
One	5.00%	90.00%	5.00%	0.00%
Two	8.47%	88.14%	3.39%	0.00%
More than two	12.50%	75.00%	12.50%	0.00%

Table 1.8 Your law school's main law review is predominantly run by whom? Broken out by ranking

Ranking	No Answer	Student	Faculty	Other
Top 20 law school	11.11%	85.19%	3.70%	0.00%
Somewhere in the 21-75 rank	3.64%	92.73%	3.64%	0.00%
76 to 250	6.52%	91.30%	2.17%	0.00%
Other	16.67%	66.67%	16.67%	0.00%

Table 1.9 Your law school's main law review is predominantly run by whom? Broken out by political views

Political views	No Answer	Student	Faculty	Other
Conservative	7.14%	92.86%	0.00%	0.00%
Centrist	8.82%	82.35%	8.82%	0.00%
Liberal	7.69%	90.77%	1.54%	0.00%
Left of Liberal	0.00%	95.00%	5.00%	0.00%
Unknown	0.00%	100.00%	0.00%	0.00%

Table 2.1 Do you believe that faculty oversight of the student run law review is too assertive, about right, or assertive enough?

	No Answer	Insufficiently assertive	About right	Assertive enough	Not really sure
Entire sample	6.72%	8.21%	61.19%	6.72%	17.16%

Table 2.2 Do you believe that faculty oversight of the student run law review is insufficiently assertive, about right, or assertive enough? Broken out by law school enrollment

Law school enrollment	No Answer	insufficiently assertive	About right	Assertive enough	Not really sure
Less than 400	12.50%	6.25%	65.63%	0.00%	15.63%
400+ - 550	3.13%	3.13%	71.88%	9.38%	12.50%
550+ - 800	2.94%	8.82%	52.94%	14.71%	20.59%
More than 800	8.33%	13.89%	55.56%	2.78%	19.44%

Table 2.3 Do you believe that faculty oversight of the student run law review is insufficiently assertive, about right, or assertive enough? Broken out by academic title

Academic title	No Answer	Insufficiently assertive	About right	Assertive enough	Not really sure
Professor	4.92%	11.48%	65.57%	4.92%	13.11%
Assistant/Associate Professor	14.29%	9.52%	33.33%	9.52%	33.33%
Adjunct/Clinical Faculty	7.14%	0.00%	60.71%	7.14%	25.00%
Emeritus	0.00%	13.33%	66.67%	13.33%	6.67%
Other	11.11%	0.00%	88.89%	0.00%	0.00%

Table 2.4 Do you believe that faculty oversight of the student run law review is insufficiently assertive, about right, or assertive enough? Broken out by age of respondent

Age of respondent	No Answer	Insufficiently assertive	About right	Assertive enough	Not really sure
Under 40	16.67%	0.00%	33.33%	16.67%	33.33%
40-49	10.53%	5.26%	52.63%	0.00%	31.58%
50-59	0.00%	6.06%	66.67%	12.12%	15.15%
60 or over	8.00%	10.67%	64.00%	5.33%	12.00%
Unknown	0.00%	0.00%	0.00%	0.00%	100.00%

Table 2.5 Do you believe that faculty oversight of the student run law review is insufficiently assertive, about right, or assertive enough? Broken out by gender of respondent

Gender of respondent	No Answer	Insufficiently assertive	About right	Assertive enough	Not really sure
Male	7.50%	11.25%	62.50%	5.00%	13.75%
Female	6.00%	4.00%	60.00%	10.00%	20.00%
Other	0.00%	0.00%	50.00%	0.00%	50.00%

Table 2.6 Do you believe that faculty oversight of the student run law review is insufficiently assertive, about right, or assertive enough? Broken out by public or private law school

Public or private law school	No Answer	Insufficiently assertive	About right	Assertive enough	Not really sure
Public	8.64%	3.70%	62.96%	6.17%	18.52%
Private	3.77%	15.09%	58.49%	7.55%	15.09%

Table 2.7 Do you believe that faculty oversight of the student run law review is insufficiently assertive, about right, or assertive enough? Broken out by # of courses taught last semester

# of courses taught last semester	No Answer	Insufficiently assertive	About right	Assertive enough	Not really sure
None	3.70%	11.11%	66.67%	7.41%	11.11%
One	2.50%	7.50%	62.50%	7.50%	20.00%
Two	10.17%	6.78%	57.63%	6.78%	18.64%
More than two	12.50%	12.50%	62.50%	0.00%	12.50%

Table 2.8 Do you believe that faculty oversight of the student run law review is insufficiently assertive, about right, or assertive enough? Broken out by ranking

Ranking	No Answer	Insufficiently assertive	About right	Assertive enough	Not really sure
Top 20 law school	11.11%	3.70%	59.26%	0.00%	25.93%
Somewhere in the 21-75 rank	1.82%	7.27%	65.45%	9.09%	16.36%
76 to 250	8.70%	13.04%	58.70%	6.52%	13.04%
Other	16.67%	0.00%	50.00%	16.67%	16.67%

Table 2.9 Do you believe that faculty oversight of the student run law review is insufficiently assertive, about right, or assertive enough? Broken out by political views

Political views	No Answer	Insufficiently assertive	About right	Assertive enough	Not really sure
Conservative	7.14%	21.43%	64.29%	0.00%	7.14%
Centrist	8.82%	11.76%	52.94%	5.88%	20.59%
Liberal	7.69%	3.08%	67.69%	10.77%	10.77%
Left of Liberal	0.00%	10.00%	55.00%	0.00%	35.00%
Unknown	0.00%	0.00%	0.00%	0.00%	100.00%

Table 3.1 How satisfied are you with the general quality of the law reviews published by your law school?

	No Answer	Very satisfied	Satisfied	Neither satisfied nor dissatisfied	Dissatisfied	Very dissatisfied
Entire sample	5.97%	11.19%	38.06%	32.84%	9.70%	2.24%

Table 3.2 How satisfied are you with the general quality of the law reviews published by your law school? Broken out by law school enrollment

Law school enrollment	No Answer	Very satisfied	Satisfied	Neither satisfied nor dissatisfied	Dissatisfied	Very dissatisfied
Less than 400	12.50%	3.13%	37.50%	34.38%	9.38%	3.13%
400+ - 550	3.13%	15.63%	43.75%	31.25%	3.13%	3.13%
550+ - 800	2.94%	11.76%	38.24%	35.29%	11.76%	0.00%
More than 800	5.56%	13.89%	33.33%	30.56%	13.89%	2.78%

Table 3.3 How satisfied are you with the general quality of the law reviews published by your law school? Broken out by academic title

Academic title	No Answer	Very satisfied	Satisfied	Neither satisfied nor dissatisfied	Dissatisfied	Very dissatisfied
Professor	4.92%	9.84%	32.79%	32.79%	18.03%	1.64%
Assistant/ Associate Professor	9.52%	4.76%	23.81%	52.38%	9.52%	0.00%
Adjunct/ Clinical Faculty	7.14%	14.29%	39.29%	32.14%	0.00%	7.14%
Emeritus	0.00%	20.00%	66.67%	13.33%	0.00%	0.00%
Other	11.11%	11.11%	55.56%	22.22%	0.00%	0.00%

Table 3.4 How satisfied are you with the general quality of the law reviews published by your law school? Broken out by age of respondent

Age of respondent	No Answer	Very satisfied	Satisfied	Neither satisfied nor dissatisfied	Dissatisfied	Very dissatisfied
Under 40	16.67%	16.67%	16.67%	50.00%	0.00%	0.00%
40-49	10.53%	10.53%	42.11%	31.58%	5.26%	0.00%
50-59	0.00%	9.09%	39.39%	42.42%	9.09%	0.00%
60 or over	6.67%	12.00%	38.67%	26.67%	12.00%	4.00%
Unknown	0.00%	0.00%	0.00%	100.00%	0.00%	0.00%

Table 3.5 How satisfied are you with the general quality of the law reviews published by your law school? Broken out by gender of respondent

Gender of respondent	No Answer	Very satisfied	Satisfied	Neither satisfied nor dissatisfied	Dissatisfied	Very dissatisfied
Male	7.50%	12.50%	38.75%	25.00%	12.50%	3.75%
Female	4.00%	10.00%	36.00%	44.00%	6.00%	0.00%
Other	0.00%	0.00%	50.00%	50.00%	0.00%	0.00%

Table 3.6 How satisfied are you with the general quality of the law reviews published by your law school? Broken out by public or private law school

Public or private law school	No Answer	Very satisfied	Satisfied	Neither satisfied nor dissatisfied	Dissatisfied	Very dissatisfied
Public	7.41%	13.58%	39.51%	27.16%	8.64%	3.70%
Private	3.77%	7.55%	35.85%	41.51%	11.32%	0.00%

Table 3.7 How satisfied are you with the general quality of the law reviews published by your law school? Broken out by # of courses taught last semester

# of courses taught last semester	No Answer	Very satisfied	Satisfied	Neither satisfied nor dissatisfied	Dissatisfied	Very dissatisfied
None	3.70%	18.52%	44.44%	25.93%	7.41%	0.00%
One	2.50%	7.50%	45.00%	35.00%	7.50%	2.50%
Two	8.47%	10.17%	32.20%	33.90%	11.86%	3.39%
More than two	12.50%	12.50%	25.00%	37.50%	12.50%	0.00%

Table 3.8 How satisfied are you with the general quality of the law reviews published by your law school? Broken out by ranking

Ranking	No Answer	Very satisfied	Satisfied	Neither satisfied nor dissatisfied	Dissatisfied	Very dissatisfied
Top 20 law school	11.11%	14.81%	37.04%	25.93%	11.11%	0.00%
Somewhere in the 21-75 rank	1.82%	18.18%	41.82%	29.09%	5.45%	3.64%
76 to 250	6.52%	2.17%	39.13%	34.78%	15.22%	2.17%
Other	16.67%	0.00%	0.00%	83.33%	0.00%	0.00%

Table 3.9 How satisfied are you with the general quality of the law reviews published by your law school? Broken out by political views

Political views	No Answer	Very satisfied	Satisfied	Neither satisfied nor dissatisfied	Dissatisfied	Very dissatisfied
Conservative	7.14%	7.14%	28.57%	21.43%	28.57%	7.14%
Centrist	8.82%	2.94%	38.24%	38.24%	8.82%	2.94%
Liberal	6.15%	15.38%	41.54%	33.85%	1.54%	1.54%
Left of Liberal	0.00%	15.00%	35.00%	30.00%	20.00%	0.00%
Unknown	0.00%	0.00%	0.00%	0.00%	100.00%	0.00%

What would you do to alter the apparent policies and priorities of your law schools law reviews?

Top 20 law school

1 Law review membership here is no longer tethered to 1L academic performance--it's now quota-driven. And these students are, predictably, imposing ideological litmus tests to article selection. The journal's contents are no longer considered serious scholarship.
2 Be more receptive to articles clarifying the law and less focused on abstract theory
3 I don't have an understanding of this as an adjunct faculty member.
4 I think their DEI policies are probably illegal.
5 Move back to a more academic focus on staff positions
6 The student law review system is what it is. Insufficiently late to displace it now, and I have no desire for a hybrid system. That quickly becomes the worst of both worlds: I have to put up with all the nonsense from student editors and I'm also expected to be a reviewer for faculty journals. No thanks. One poison is enough.
7 Articles insufficiently abstract and not practical. Never cited in court.
8 Insufficient knowledge

Somewhere in the 21-75 rank

1 No opinion
2 I would not alter the current policies.
3 To do it right would require the investment of significant Faculty resources. Instead of proliferating journals, faculties should be engaged in more hands-on training of students in writing.
4 Law reviews are a strange breed, but legal scholarship is weird too. As long as the citation form is followed, who cares?
5 Undo the current editorial board's policy that permits students to satisfy their note requirement using AI as long as they are not seeking publication.
6 I don't have any knowledge about law reviews
7 I would only add a mandate that they receive credit ONLY if they publish their editions on time each year.
8 More faculty involvement
9 More training in quality research and writing skills
10 More faculty input
11 No comment
12 Anti racist agendas don't sufficiently protect academic freedom of authors
13 Peer review
14 Nothing
15 I am unfamiliar with the policies.

16 I think 2L law review selection generally perpetuates the status quo of 1L learning rather than of sophisticated legal academic thought. 2Ls are too invested in changing the law review submission and selection procedure because the law review is hard and their time is short. when law reviews are cited by courts to change or maintain policy and doctrine, this 1L mentality of "what the law is" or "what the law should be" is subject to the lowest common denominator. It's a real problem when what counts as excellent legal scholarship is decided by law students with 3 semesters of law school under their belt.
17 More faculty involvement in choosing articles
18 Don't know
19 Integrate more peer review.
20 I'm not sure what the survey means by apparent policies
21 I am unsure.
22 We shouldn't have the secondary ones; the flagship is good.
23 Nothing.
24 I don't have a problem with the school's direction.
25 Include more inquiry into diversity of authors and subject matter that is intending to bring critical lenses to the law.
26 Replace with peer reviewed journals
27 Try to enlist more faculty participation and support for law reviews.
28 Introduce peer review

76 to 250

1 Law reviews should address specific issues that help practitioners in their jurisdiction or area of expertise.
2 Ugh. Law reviews. They are just silly most of the time to me. Most of the articles are useless. The useful ones are too long. The students don't have enough supervision to learn to really cute or edit well, but I don't see how we can fund that kind of intensive supervision. Many probably actually become worse writers and editors through this experience. But it does give authors tons of publishers to get their work through, and students get artificially prestigious resume padding. So I guess that's helpful?
3 Nothing
4 Greater professor involvement/direction provided.
5 Would make the review more relevant to our environment and setting.
6 Nothing
7 Greater resources would allow the students more latitude to experiment and grow content, to attract talented guests to symposia, to afford students better preparation and training, and to afford students more time to do the work, vis-a-vis other priorities such as paid employment. Seems to me that everyone's priorities are in the right place and on the same page, but you can do only so much with a shoestring operation.
8 We have a second journal, and I question the quality of the staff and output from that journal.

9 Build in more expectation of consultation with faculty about articles received.
10 I'd eliminate our racial preferences to join.
11 None
12 Keep their independence
13 In infusion of national and international perspective and intellectual depth. With the exception of an online journal published once a year, the product is grossly provincial on par with a state bar publication. Faculty influence over student writing projects is too strong given the faculty do not invest the time and effort providing elevating feedback.
14 It is not a problem of priorities or policies. It is a problem of journalistic and intellectual rigor.
15 I would have the second year students write shorter pieces so more of them can get published.
16 Nothing, not really my focus
17 The students need much more guidance and instruction on the scholarly process and how to engage with academic scholars.
18 I don't pay close enough attention to comment
19 Not sure.

Other

1 I do not know

Table 4.1 Do you believe that ethnic, racial or gender balance should be a consideration in the selection of law school editors?

	No Answer	Yes	No
Entire sample	13.43%	31.34%	55.22%

Table 4.2 Do you believe that ethnic, racial or gender balance should be a consideration in the selection of law school editors? Broken out by law school enrollment

Law school enrollment	No Answer	Yes	No
Less than 400	28.13%	9.38%	62.50%
400+ - 550	6.25%	34.38%	59.38%
550+ - 800	14.71%	41.18%	44.12%
More than 800	5.56%	38.89%	55.56%

Table 4.3 Do you believe that ethnic, racial or gender balance should be a consideration in the selection of law school editors? Broken out by academic title

Academic title	No Answer	Yes	No
Professor	13.11%	24.59%	62.30%
Assistant/Associate Professor	23.81%	52.38%	23.81%
Adjunct/Clinical Faculty	14.29%	35.71%	50.00%
Emeritus	0.00%	26.67%	73.33%
Other	11.11%	22.22%	66.67%

Table 4.4 Do you believe that ethnic, racial or gender balance should be a consideration in the selection of law school editors? Broken out by age of respondent

Age of respondent	No Answer	Yes	No
Under 40	16.67%	66.67%	16.67%
40-49	15.79%	42.11%	42.11%
50-59	12.12%	48.48%	39.39%
60 or over	12.00%	18.67%	69.33%
Unknown	100.00%	0.00%	0.00%

Table 4.5 Do you believe that ethnic, racial or gender balance should be a consideration in the selection of law school editors? Broken out by gender of respondent

Gender of respondent	No Answer	Yes	No
Male	13.75%	21.25%	65.00%
Female	10.00%	48.00%	42.00%
Other	50.00%	25.00%	25.00%

Table 4.6 Do you believe that ethnic, racial or gender balance should be a consideration in the selection of law school editors? Broken out by public or private law school

Public or private law school	No Answer	Yes	No
Public	16.05%	30.86%	53.09%
Private	9.43%	32.08%	58.49%

Table 4.7 Do you believe that ethnic, racial or gender balance should be a consideration in the selection of law school editors? Broken out by # of courses taught last semester

# of courses taught last semester	No Answer	Yes	No
None	3.70%	37.04%	59.26%
One	12.50%	37.50%	50.00%
Two	15.25%	22.03%	62.71%
More than two	37.50%	50.00%	12.50%

Table 4.8 Do you believe that ethnic, racial or gender balance should be a consideration in the selection of law school editors? Broken out by ranking

Ranking	No Answer	Yes	No
Top 20 law school	11.11%	37.04%	51.85%
Somewhere in the 21-75 rank	12.73%	27.27%	60.00%
76 to 250	13.04%	30.43%	56.52%
Other	33.33%	50.00%	16.67%

Table 4.9 Do you believe that ethnic, racial or gender balance should be a consideration in the selection of law school editors? Broken out by political views

Political views	No Answer	Yes	No
Conservative	7.14%	14.29%	78.57%
Centrist	14.71%	11.76%	73.53%
Liberal	13.85%	38.46%	47.69%
Left of Liberal	15.00%	55.00%	30.00%
Unknown	0.00%	0.00%	100.00%

Table 5 Have you served in any of the following capacities for any specialty or other type of law review published by your law school?

Table 5.1.1 Have you served in any of the following capacities for any specialty or other type of law review published by your law school? Editor.

	No Answer	Yes	No
Entire sample	0.00%	8.21%	91.79%

Table 5.1.2 Have you served in any of the following capacities for any specialty or other type of law review published by your law school? Editor. Broken out by law school enrollment

Law school enrollment	Yes	No
Less than 400	9.38%	90.63%
400+ - 550	12.50%	87.50%
550+ - 800	2.94%	97.06%
More than 800	8.33%	91.67%

Table 5.1.3 Have you served in any of the following capacities for any specialty or other type of law review published by your law school? Editor. Broken out by academic title

Academic title	Yes	No
Professor	4.92%	95.08%
Assistant/Associate Professor	4.76%	95.24%
Adjunct/Clinical Faculty	17.86%	82.14%
Emeritus	6.67%	93.33%
Other	11.11%	88.89%

Table 5.1.4 Have you served in any of the following capacities for any specialty or other type of law review published by your law school? Editor. Broken out by age of respondent

Age of respondent	Yes	No
Under 40	16.67%	83.33%
40-49	0.00%	100.00%
50-59	6.06%	93.94%
60 or over	10.67%	89.33%
Unknown	0.00%	100.00%

Table 5.1.5 Have you served in any of the following capacities for any specialty or other type of law review published by your law school? Editor. Broken out by gender of respondent

Gender of respondent	Yes	No
Male	8.75%	91.25%
Female	8.00%	92.00%
Other	0.00%	100.00%

Table 5.1.6 Have you served in any of the following capacities for any specialty or other type of law review published by your law school? Editor. Broken out by public or private law school

Public or private law school	Yes	No
Public	9.88%	90.12%
Private	5.66%	94.34%

Table 5.1.7 Have you served in any of the following capacities for any specialty or other type of law review published by your law school? Editor. Broken out by # of courses taught last semester

# of courses taught last semester	Yes	No
None	11.11%	88.89%
One	2.50%	97.50%
Two	11.86%	88.14%
More than two	0.00%	100.00%

Table 5.1.8 Have you served in any of the following capacities for any specialty or other type of law review published by your law school? Editor. Broken out by ranking

Ranking	Yes	No
Top 20 law school	14.81%	85.19%
Somewhere in the 21-75 rank	5.45%	94.55%
76 to 250	8.70%	91.30%
Other	0.00%	100.00%

Table 5.1.9 Have you served in any of the following capacities for any specialty or other type of law review published by your law school? Editor. Broken out by political views

Political views	Yes	No
Conservative	21.43%	78.57%
Centrist	14.71%	85.29%
Liberal	4.62%	95.38%
Left of Liberal	0.00%	100.00%
Unknown	0.00%	100.00%

Table 5.2.1 Have you served in any of the following capacities for any specialty or other type of law review published by your law school? Peer Reviewer.

	No Answer	Yes	No
Entire sample	0.00%	17.16%	82.84%

Table 5.2.2 Have you served in any of the following capacities for any specialty or other type of law review published by your law school? Peer Reviewer. Broken out by law school enrollment

Law school enrollment	Yes	No
Less than 400	6.25%	93.75%
400+ - 550	15.63%	84.38%
550+ - 800	29.41%	70.59%
More than 800	16.67%	83.33%

Table 5.2.3 Have you served in any of the following capacities for any specialty or other type of law review published by your law school? Peer Reviewer. Broken out by academic title

Academic title	Yes	No
Professor	21.31%	78.69%
Assistant/Associate Professor	14.29%	85.71%
Adjunct/Clinical Faculty	7.14%	92.86%
Emeritus	33.33%	66.67%
Other	0.00%	100.00%

Table 5.2.4 Have you served in any of the following capacities for any specialty or other type of law review published by your law school? Peer Reviewer. Broken out by age of respondent

Age of respondent	Yes	No
Under 40	16.67%	83.33%
40-49	5.26%	94.74%
50-59	18.18%	81.82%
60 or over	18.67%	81.33%
Unknown	100.00%	0.00%

Table 5.2.5 Have you served in any of the following capacities for any specialty or other type of law review published by your law school? Peer Reviewer. Broken out by gender of respondent

Gender of respondent	Yes	No
Male	12.50%	87.50%
Female	24.00%	76.00%
Other	25.00%	75.00%

Table 5.2.6 Have you served in any of the following capacities for any specialty or other type of law review published by your law school? Peer Reviewer. Broken out by public or private law school

Public or private law school	Yes	No
Public	13.58%	86.42%
Private	22.64%	77.36%

Table 5.2.7 Have you served in any of the following capacities for any specialty or other type of law review published by your law school? Peer Reviewer. Broken out by # of courses taught last semester

# of courses taught last semester	Yes	No
None	22.22%	77.78%
One	15.00%	85.00%
Two	18.64%	81.36%
More than two	0.00%	100.00%

Table 5.2.8 Have you served in any of the following capacities for any specialty or other type of law review published by your law school? Peer Reviewer. Broken out by ranking

Ranking	Yes	No
Top 20 law school	11.11%	88.89%
Somewhere in the 21-75 rank	20.00%	80.00%
76 to 250	19.57%	80.43%
Other	0.00%	100.00%

Table 5.2.9 Have you served in any of the following capacities for any specialty or other type of law review published by your law school? Peer Reviewer. Broken out by political views

Political views	Yes	No
Conservative	21.43%	78.57%
Centrist	11.76%	88.24%
Liberal	24.62%	75.38%
Left of Liberal	0.00%	100.00%
Unknown	0.00%	100.00%

Table 5.3.1 Have you served in any of the following capacities for any specialty or other type of law review published by your law school? Contributor.

	No Answer	Yes	No
Entire sample	0.00%	22.39%	77.61%

Table 5.3.2 Have you served in any of the following capacities for any specialty or other type of law review published by your law school? Contributor. Broken out by law school enrollment

Law school enrollment	Yes	No
Less than 400	15.63%	84.38%
400+ - 550	18.75%	81.25%
550+ - 800	29.41%	70.59%
More than 800	25.00%	75.00%

Table 5.3.3 Have you served in any of the following capacities for any specialty or other type of law review published by your law school? Contributor. Broken out by academic title

Academic title	Yes	No
Professor	27.87%	72.13%
Assistant/Associate Professor	0.00%	100.00%
Adjunct/Clinical Faculty	14.29%	85.71%
Emeritus	46.67%	53.33%
Other	22.22%	77.78%

Table 5.3.4 Have you served in any of the following capacities for any specialty or other type of law review published by your law school? Contributor. Broken out by age of respondent

Age of respondent	Yes	No
Under 40	0.00%	100.00%
40-49	5.26%	94.74%
50-59	12.12%	87.88%
60 or over	33.33%	66.67%
Unknown	0.00%	100.00%

Table 5.3.5 Have you served in any of the following capacities for any specialty or other type of law review published by your law school? Contributor. Broken out by gender of respondent

Gender of respondent	Yes	No
Male	26.25%	73.75%
Female	18.00%	82.00%
Other	0.00%	100.00%

Table 5.3.6 Have you served in any of the following capacities for any specialty or other type of law review published by your law school? Contributor. Broken out by public or private law school

Public or private law school	Yes	No
Public	19.75%	80.25%
Private	26.42%	73.58%

Table 5.3.7 Have you served in any of the following capacities for any specialty or other type of law review published by your law school? Contributor. Broken out by # of courses taught last semester

# of courses taught last semester	Yes	No
None	33.33%	66.67%
One	17.50%	82.50%
Two	20.34%	79.66%
More than two	25.00%	75.00%

Table 5.3.8 Have you served in any of the following capacities for any specialty or other type of law review published by your law school? Contributor. Broken out by ranking

Ranking	Yes	No
Top 20 law school	25.93%	74.07%
Somewhere in the 21-75 rank	21.82%	78.18%
76 to 250	21.74%	78.26%
Other	16.67%	83.33%

Table 5.3.9 Have you served in any of the following capacities for any specialty or other type of law review published by your law school? Contributor. Broken out by political views

Political views	Yes	No
Conservative	64.29%	35.71%
Centrist	23.53%	76.47%
Liberal	18.46%	81.54%
Left of Liberal	5.00%	95.00%
Unknown	0.00%	100.00%

Table 5.4.1 Have you served in any of the following capacities for any specialty or other type of law review published by your law school? Faculty Advisor.

	No Answer	Yes	No
Entire sample	0.00%	25.37%	74.63%

Table 5.4.2 Have you served in any of the following capacities for any specialty or other type of law review published by your law school? Faculty Advisor. Broken out by law school enrollment

Law school enrollment	Yes	No
Less than 400	12.50%	87.50%
400+ - 550	37.50%	62.50%
550+ - 800	23.53%	76.47%
More than 800	27.78%	72.22%

Table 5.4.3 Have you served in any of the following capacities for any specialty or other type of law review published by your law school? Faculty Advisor. Broken out by academic title

Academic title	Yes	No
Professor	40.98%	59.02%
Assistant/Associate Professor	4.76%	95.24%
Adjunct/Clinical Faculty	3.57%	96.43%
Emeritus	40.00%	60.00%
Other	11.11%	88.89%

Table 5.4.4 Have you served in any of the following capacities for any specialty or other type of law review published by your law school? Faculty Advisor. Broken out by age of respondent

Age of respondent	Yes	No
Under 40	0.00%	100.00%
40-49	26.32%	73.68%
50-59	24.24%	75.76%
60 or over	28.00%	72.00%
Unknown	0.00%	100.00%

Table 5.4.5 Have you served in any of the following capacities for any specialty or other type of law review published by your law school? Faculty Advisor. Broken out by gender of respondent

Gender of respondent	Yes	No
Male	26.25%	73.75%
Female	26.00%	74.00%
Other	0.00%	100.00%

Table 5.4.6 Have you served in any of the following capacities for any specialty or other type of law review published by your law school? Faculty Advisor. Broken out by public or private law school

Public or private law school	Yes	No
Public	23.46%	76.54%
Private	28.30%	71.70%

Table 5.4.7 Have you served in any of the following capacities for any specialty or other type of law review published by your law school? Faculty Advisor. Broken out by # of courses taught last semester

# of courses taught last semester	Yes	No
None	22.22%	77.78%
One	22.50%	77.50%
Two	30.51%	69.49%
More than two	12.50%	87.50%

Table 5.4.8 Have you served in any of the following capacities for any specialty or other type of law review published by your law school? Faculty Advisor. Broken out by ranking

Ranking	Yes	No
Top 20 law school	11.11%	88.89%
Somewhere in the 21-75 rank	36.36%	63.64%
76 to 250	21.74%	78.26%
Other	16.67%	83.33%

Table 5.4.9 Have you served in any of the following capacities for any specialty or other type of law review published by your law school? Faculty Advisor. Broken out by political views

Political views	Yes	No
Conservative	28.57%	71.43%
Centrist	14.71%	85.29%
Liberal	30.77%	69.23%
Left of Liberal	25.00%	75.00%
Unknown	0.00%	100.00%

Table 6.1 About how desirable do you feel it would be to work as a faculty advisor to your law school's main law review?

	No Answer	Extremely desirable	Very desirable	Somewhat desirable	Not so desirable	Not at all desirable
Entire sample	8.21%	2.99%	4.48%	35.82%	31.34%	17.16%

Table 6.2 About how desirable do you feel it would be to work as a faculty advisor to your law school's main law review? Broken out by law school enrollment

Law school enrollment	No Answer	Extremely desirable	Very desirable	Somewhat desirable	Not so desirable	Not at all desirable
Less than 400	15.63%	3.13%	9.38%	31.25%	25.00%	15.63%
400+ - 550	6.25%	6.25%	6.25%	37.50%	31.25%	12.50%
550+ - 800	5.88%	0.00%	2.94%	44.12%	32.35%	14.71%
More than 800	5.56%	2.78%	0.00%	30.56%	36.11%	25.00%

Table 6.3 About how desirable do you feel it would be to work as a faculty advisor to your law school's main law review? Broken out by academic title

Academic title	No Answer	Extremely desirable	Very desirable	Somewhat desirable	Not so desirable	Not at all desirable
Professor	6.56%	0.00%	3.28%	36.07%	37.70%	16.39%
Assistant/ Associate Professor	14.29%	0.00%	9.52%	33.33%	38.10%	4.76%
Adjunct/ Clinical Faculty	10.71%	3.57%	0.00%	39.29%	28.57%	17.86%
Emeritus	0.00%	20.00%	6.67%	33.33%	20.00%	20.00%
Other	11.11%	0.00%	11.11%	33.33%	0.00%	44.44%

Table 6.4 About how desirable do you feel it would be to work as a faculty advisor to your law school's main law review? Broken out by age of respondent

Age of respondent	No Answer	Extremely desirable	Very desirable	Somewhat desirable	Not so desirable	Not at all desirable
Under 40	16.67%	0.00%	0.00%	33.33%	50.00%	0.00%
40-49	15.79%	0.00%	5.26%	31.58%	26.32%	21.05%
50-59	0.00%	0.00%	6.06%	33.33%	51.52%	9.09%
60 or over	9.33%	5.33%	4.00%	37.33%	22.67%	21.33%
Unknown	0.00%	0.00%	0.00%	100.00%	0.00%	0.00%

Table 6.5 About how desirable do you feel it would be to work as a faculty advisor to your law school's main law review? Broken out by gender of respondent

Gender of respondent	No Answer	Extremely desirable	Very desirable	Somewhat desirable	Not so desirable	Not at all desirable
Male	7.50%	5.00%	6.25%	36.25%	23.75%	21.25%
Female	6.00%	0.00%	2.00%	36.00%	46.00%	10.00%
Other	50.00%	0.00%	0.00%	25.00%	0.00%	25.00%

Table 6.6 About how desirable do you feel it would be to work as a faculty advisor to your law school's main law review? Broken out by public or private law school

Public or private law school	No Answer	Extremely desirable	Very desirable	Somewhat desirable	Not so desirable	Not at all desirable
Public	8.64%	3.70%	3.70%	35.80%	29.63%	18.52%
Private	7.55%	1.89%	5.66%	35.85%	33.96%	15.09%

Table 6.7 About how desirable do you feel it would be to work as a faculty advisor to your law school's main law review? Broken out by # of courses taught last semester

# of courses taught last semester	No Answer	Extremely desirable	Very desirable	Somewhat desirable	Not so desirable	Not at all desirable
None	3.70%	11.11%	3.70%	44.44%	14.81%	22.22%
One	5.00%	0.00%	0.00%	40.00%	35.00%	20.00%
Two	6.78%	1.69%	8.47%	32.20%	37.29%	13.56%
More than two	50.00%	0.00%	0.00%	12.50%	25.00%	12.50%

Table 6.8 About how desirable do you feel it would be to work as a faculty advisor to your law school's main law review? Broken out by ranking

Ranking	No Answer	Extremely desirable	Very desirable	Somewhat desirable	Not so desirable	Not at all desirable
Top 20 law school	14.81%	0.00%	0.00%	33.33%	25.93%	25.93%
Somewhere in the 21-75 rank	5.45%	5.45%	3.64%	50.91%	23.64%	10.91%
76 to 250	4.35%	2.17%	8.70%	23.91%	39.13%	21.74%
Other	33.33%	0.00%	0.00%	0.00%	66.67%	0.00%

Table 6.9 About how desirable do you feel it would be to work as a faculty advisor to your law school's main law review? Broken out by political views

Political views	No Answer	Extremely desirable	Very desirable	Somewhat desirable	Not so desirable	Not at all desirable
Conservative	7.14%	0.00%	0.00%	28.57%	42.86%	21.43%
Centrist	8.82%	2.94%	11.76%	44.12%	23.53%	8.82%
Liberal	7.69%	3.08%	1.54%	36.92%	33.85%	16.92%
Left of Liberal	10.00%	5.00%	5.00%	25.00%	30.00%	25.00%
Unknown	0.00%	0.00%	0.00%	0.00%	0.00%	100.00%

Table 7.1 How fair is the selection criteria and process for selecting law review editors from the student body?

	No Answer	Very Fair	Generally Fair	Sometimes Fair	Often Unfair	Very Unfair
Entire sample	21.64%	10.45%	50.75%	11.94%	2.99%	2.24%

Table 7.2 How fair is the selection criteria and process for selecting law review editors from the student body? Broken out by law school enrollment

Law school enrollment	No Answer	Very Fair	Generally Fair	Sometimes Fair	Often Unfair	Very Unfair
Less than 400	28.13%	18.75%	43.75%	6.25%	0.00%	3.13%
400+ - 550	15.63%	12.50%	56.25%	9.38%	3.13%	3.13%
550+ - 800	20.59%	5.88%	55.88%	11.76%	2.94%	2.94%
More than 800	22.22%	5.56%	47.22%	19.44%	5.56%	0.00%

Table 7.3 How fair is the selection criteria and process for selecting law review editors from the student body? Broken out by academic title

Academic title	No Answer	Very Fair	Generally Fair	Sometimes Fair	Often Unfair	Very Unfair
Professor	16.39%	14.75%	49.18%	11.48%	4.92%	3.28%
Assistant/ Associate Professor	23.81%	0.00%	52.38%	19.05%	4.76%	0.00%
Adjunct/ Clinical Faculty	42.86%	3.57%	42.86%	7.14%	0.00%	3.57%
Emeritus	6.67%	13.33%	66.67%	13.33%	0.00%	0.00%
Other	11.11%	22.22%	55.56%	11.11%	0.00%	0.00%

Table 7.4 How fair is the selection criteria and process for selecting law review editors from the student body? Broken out by age of respondent

Age of respondent	No Answer	Very Fair	Generally Fair	Sometimes Fair	Often Unfair	Very Unfair
Under 40	50.00%	0.00%	33.33%	16.67%	0.00%	0.00%
40-49	42.11%	5.26%	36.84%	15.79%	0.00%	0.00%
50-59	9.09%	9.09%	66.67%	12.12%	0.00%	3.03%
60 or over	20.00%	13.33%	48.00%	10.67%	5.33%	2.67%
Unknown	0.00%	0.00%	100.00%	0.00%	0.00%	0.00%

Table 7.5 How fair is the selection criteria and process for selecting law review editors from the student body? Broken out by gender of respondent

Gender of respondent	No Answer	Very Fair	Generally Fair	Sometimes Fair	Often Unfair	Very Unfair
Male	18.75%	12.50%	51.25%	11.25%	3.75%	2.50%
Female	22.00%	8.00%	52.00%	14.00%	2.00%	2.00%
Other	75.00%	0.00%	25.00%	0.00%	0.00%	0.00%

Table 7.6 How fair is the selection criteria and process for selecting law review editors from the student body? Broken out by public or private law school

Public or private law school	No Answer	Very Fair	Generally Fair	Sometimes Fair	Often Unfair	Very Unfair
Public	24.69%	11.11%	49.38%	9.88%	3.70%	1.23%
Private	16.98%	9.43%	52.83%	15.09%	1.89%	3.77%

Table 7.7 How fair is the selection criteria and process for selecting law review editors from the student body? Broken out by # of courses taught last semester

# of courses taught last semester	No Answer	Very Fair	Generally Fair	Sometimes Fair	Often Unfair	Very Unfair
None	11.11%	11.11%	51.85%	25.93%	0.00%	0.00%
One	22.50%	2.50%	57.50%	7.50%	5.00%	5.00%
Two	20.34%	15.25%	52.54%	6.78%	3.39%	1.69%
More than two	62.50%	12.50%	0.00%	25.00%	0.00%	0.00%

Table 7.8 How fair is the selection criteria and process for selecting law review editors from the student body? Broken out by ranking

Ranking	No Answer	Very Fair	Generally Fair	Sometimes Fair	Often Unfair	Very Unfair
Top 20 law school	37.04%	0.00%	44.44%	11.11%	3.70%	3.70%
Somewhere in the 21-75 rank	16.36%	12.73%	52.73%	12.73%	1.82%	3.64%
76 to 250	15.22%	13.04%	56.52%	10.87%	4.35%	0.00%
Other	50.00%	16.67%	16.67%	16.67%	0.00%	0.00%

Table 7.9 How fair is the selection criteria and process for selecting law review editors from the student body? Broken out by political views

Political views	No Answer	Very Fair	Generally Fair	Sometimes Fair	Often Unfair	Very Unfair
Conservative	14.29%	7.14%	42.86%	21.43%	14.29%	0.00%
Centrist	23.53%	11.76%	41.18%	20.59%	2.94%	0.00%
Liberal	18.46%	12.31%	63.08%	1.54%	1.54%	3.08%
Left of Liberal	30.00%	5.00%	35.00%	25.00%	0.00%	5.00%
Unknown	100.00%	0.00%	0.00%	0.00%	0.00%	0.00%

Survey of Law School Faculty 2025, Evaluating the Law Review

What would make your law school's law review better?

Top 20 law school

1 Make selection purely based on blinded academic performance.
2 More focus on issues of importance to the profession
3 I don't know enough about it.
4 More meritocratic selection with a greater emphasis on grades
5 Concrete, Practical, Real world
6 Insufficient knowledge

Somewhere in the 21-75 rank

1 No opinion
2 The product is fine, but the student experience is lacking because they do too much busy work re citations etc.
3 More diversity
4 A greater emphasis on social science approaches
5 Convincing a greater number of students of the value proposition of spending the time to write on and, if successful, to participate more fully in law review as opposed to looking outside the law school for part-time work as a clerk for some ambulance chaser.
6 Not my job, student run.
7 I don't have much knowledge of law review
8 Attract more widely-known scholars or articles on more "topical" subjects. Organize symposia regularly.
9 Supervision
10 Terrific candidates have been selected, but it's often a popularity contest in part
11 More accountability to the faculty
12 Peer review
13 More peer review, less elitism in the selection process
14 Moving up in the rankings
15 Not certain is also the answer for 34
16 Peer review of articles rather than student selection.
17 More faculty input in article selection.
18 No thoughts
19 I don't feel qualified to answer this question.
20 Increase voluntary faculty participation in reviewing articles.
21 Base it on a more honest competition

76 to 250

1 Write things lawyers can actually use.
2 I struggle to see how we could make significant changes within the current law review and law school system. I would try to get the students in more meaningful communication with the authors.
3 Willingness of faculty at higher ranked schools to publish here
4 Better quality article selection.

5 See above.
6 Better funding
7 Money.
8 Many top students work at big law firms in town and choose not to participate on the law review. I think it is unfortunate that they choose to forego that opportunity. I don't have a solution to that besides better marketing of the value of the law review experience.
9 A full-time staff member dedicated to the law review.
10 Publish 3, not 4, issues.
11 I don't know.
12 Refocusing on grades and scholarship
13 More reliance on law school grades for membership
14 Smarter students
15 Open vision to extend beyond the state's borders and priority issues within the jurisdiction. It is, at its core, a state bar publication with more ambitious research and citation.
16 Higher standards
17 See above
18 No idea
19 Better advising, better process. The sequence of assignment submissions makes no sense for law review students working on their notes. They are asked to submit drafts too early and without the benefit of periodic review and check-ins to ensure sound process. The students are capable, but they don't know what to do until it is too late to course correct.
20 More symposia on real law subjects.
21 I don't pay close enough attention to comment

Table 8.1 As best as you can ascertain, how effective is your law school in assuring that the law schools law reviews are effectively marketed and available in various formats and venues?

	No Answer	Extremely effective	Very effective	Somewhat effective	Not so effective	Not at all effective
Entire sample	17.91%	2.99%	17.16%	44.78%	13.43%	3.73%

Table 8.2 As best as you can ascertain how effective is your law school in assuring that the law schools law reviews are effectively marketed and available in various formats and venues? Broken out by law school enrollment

Law school enrollment	No Answer	Extremely effective	Very effective	Somewhat effective	Not so effective	Not at all effective
Less than 400	28.13%	0.00%	15.63%	37.50%	12.50%	6.25%
400+ - 550	12.50%	3.13%	21.88%	43.75%	15.63%	3.13%
550+ - 800	14.71%	5.88%	14.71%	44.12%	14.71%	5.88%
More than 800	16.67%	2.78%	16.67%	52.78%	11.11%	0.00%

Table 8.3 As best as you can ascertain, how effective is your law school in assuring that the law schools law reviews are effectively marketed and available in various formats and venues? Broken out by academic title

Academic title	No Answer	Extremely effective	Very effective	Somewhat effective	Not so effective	Not at all effective
Professor	14.75%	1.64%	19.67%	50.82%	9.84%	3.28%
Assistant/ Associate Professor	23.81%	0.00%	9.52%	42.86%	23.81%	0.00%
Adjunct/ Clinical Faculty	28.57%	7.14%	14.29%	32.14%	10.71%	7.14%
Emeritus	6.67%	0.00%	20.00%	46.67%	20.00%	6.67%
Other	11.11%	11.11%	22.22%	44.44%	11.11%	0.00%

Table 8.4 As best as you can ascertain, how effective is your law school in assuring that the law schools law reviews are effectively marketed and available in various formats and venues? Broken out by age of respondent

Age of respondent	No Answer	Extremely effective	Very effective	Somewhat effective	Not so effective	Not at all effective
Under 40	50.00%	0.00%	16.67%	0.00%	33.33%	0.00%
40-49	31.58%	5.26%	21.05%	36.84%	5.26%	0.00%
50-59	6.06%	6.06%	15.15%	57.58%	12.12%	3.03%
60 or over	17.33%	1.33%	17.33%	45.33%	13.33%	5.33%
Unknown	0.00%	0.00%	0.00%	0.00%	100.00%	0.00%

Table 8.5 As best as you can ascertain how effective is your law school in assuring that the law schools law reviews are effectively marketed and available in various formats and venues? Broken out by gender of respondent

Gender of respondent	No Answer	Extremely effective	Very effective	Somewhat effective	Not so effective	Not at all effective
Male	16.25%	2.50%	17.50%	48.75%	10.00%	5.00%
Female	16.00%	4.00%	18.00%	42.00%	18.00%	2.00%
Other	75.00%	0.00%	0.00%	0.00%	25.00%	0.00%

Table 8.6 As best as you can ascertain, how effective is your law school in assuring that the law schools law reviews are effectively marketed and available in various formats and venues? Broken out by public or private law school

Public or private law school	No Answer	Extremely effective	Very effective	Somewhat effective	Not so effective	Not at all effective
Public	19.75%	3.70%	17.28%	40.74%	13.58%	4.94%
Private	15.09%	1.89%	16.98%	50.94%	13.21%	1.89%

Table 8.7 As best as you can ascertain, how effective is your law school in assuring that the law schools law reviews are effectively marketed and available in various formats and venues? Broken out by # of courses taught last semester

# of courses taught last semester	No Answer	Extremely effective	Very effective	Somewhat effective	Not so effective	Not at all effective
None	11.11%	7.41%	14.81%	44.44%	18.52%	3.70%
One	15.00%	5.00%	15.00%	60.00%	5.00%	0.00%
Two	16.95%	0.00%	22.03%	37.29%	18.64%	5.08%
More than two	62.50%	0.00%	0.00%	25.00%	0.00%	12.50%

Table 8.8 As best as you can ascertain, how effective is your law school in assuring that the law schools law reviews are effectively marketed and available in various formats and venues? Broken out by ranking

Ranking	No Answer	Extremely effective	Very effective	Somewhat effective	Not so effective	Not at all effective
Top 20 law school	37.04%	7.41%	11.11%	37.04%	7.41%	0.00%
Somewhere in the 21-75 rank	10.91%	3.64%	20.00%	49.09%	12.73%	3.64%
76 to 250	10.87%	0.00%	19.57%	45.65%	17.39%	6.52%
Other	50.00%	0.00%	0.00%	33.33%	16.67%	0.00%

Table 8.9 As best as you can ascertain, how effective is your law school in assuring that the law schools law reviews are effectively marketed and available in various formats and venues? Broken out by political views

Political views	No Answer	Extremely effective	Very effective	Somewhat effective	Not so effective	Not at all effective
Conservative	14.29%	7.14%	14.29%	50.00%	7.14%	7.14%
Centrist	17.65%	0.00%	11.76%	55.88%	11.76%	2.94%
Liberal	16.92%	3.08%	21.54%	38.46%	16.92%	3.08%
Left of Liberal	25.00%	5.00%	15.00%	40.00%	10.00%	5.00%
Unknown	0.00%	0.00%	0.00%	100.00%	0.00%	0.00%